James in-depth study guide

I'll follow You, no matter the cost.

James 1:2-4

We all fall into various trials. Sickness, divorce, anxiety, depression, foreclosure, death, loss of income, etc. This verse tells us to take great pleasure in these trials. Not because they are easy, but because of what they produce.

For example, when you lose your job, you have a choice. Do you panic, scream, get mad at God for allowing it to happen, etc, or do you trust Him? Do you have faith, even in really hard, and what feels like unbearable circumstances?

Your faith produces patience. It means having patience and faith, knowing that you'll find another job, knowing that God is in control, and that His will be done, even if it hurts.

Trusting God says, "I'll follow you, no matter the cost".

I don't speak these words lightly, because it's far from being easy. But even if you start rocky and doubtful, don't end there. This is what helps you build endurance for the race marked out for you through Christ Jesus. This is what produces patience and faith building.

If I were to work out everyday for a year, are the results instant? No, they take time. Time to build that muscle. So working on it daily, gains strength, and as time goes on, more endurance. You may start out not wanting to work out everyday, but over time, you build patience, drive, and perseverance to do what you set out to do.

In the same way, testing of your faith works the same way. Just as waking up everyday and pushing yourself to work out is hard, so is waking up every day and relying on God's strength to get you through that day, no matter what it may bring. It takes time, faith, and patience. But if you stick with it, your faith will grow stronger and less and less doubtful of what lies ahead.

James 1:5-8

Wisdom is crucial in the Christian walk.

She is more precious than rubies, And all the things you may desire cannot compare with her.

Proverbs 3:15

For wisdom is better than rubies, And all the things one may desire cannot be compared with her.

Proverbs 8:11

How much better to get wisdom than gold!

Proverbs 16:16

Wisdom is better than strength.

Ecclesiastes 9:16

Wisdom is better than weapons of war

Ecclesiastes 9:18

So as you see, you need wisdom. Wisdom guides you, helps you make the wisest decisions, wisdom paths are all peace, and she is needed in the Christian life. Sometimes our thoughts cloud our judgment. We feel sad so we have a hard time picking which path to take, we have anxiety so all the paths seem cloudy and unsure, and we get scared of choosing a path, so we choose none. We then end up stagnant because we can't make a decision. This is where wisdom comes in. God is smart, He thought of everything. He knew that we would need wisdom, and we need to realize this too. You can avoid a lot of mistakes and pitfalls in life by relying on wisdom. If you feel like you need more wisdom, guess what? All you have to do is ask. Yes, it's that simple. In life, we tend to not get the things that we ask for. We are programmed by human standards to say that it's not as easy as asking for help or asking for guidance. We forget at times, God's not like us. He enjoys giving us things that we ask for, He loves making us happy, and answering our prayers. God's not stingy with His offerings and doesn't hoard what He owns. Hes giving, loving, and pure. This is why He tells us here to ask for wisdom and it will be given to you. Literally, just ask. But make no mistake, you have a part to play here as well. Your part is simple. Just believe. Don't doubt. If you doubt you are like a wave that tosses to and fro. The slightest gust of wind can produce a wave. Don't let every negative thing that comes your way, move you. Stand firm in the Lord and believe, and do not doubt. If you do, this verse tells you that you shouldn't expect to receive anything from the Lord. This is because when you doubt, you are like a wave in the ocean, which moves to and fro with every blow of wind. Don't be so quickly moved by the winds and waves of your life. Every trial, every worry, every stress. Let it all go and place it in the hands of your loving Father. Once you fully let go, you will realize that it was never your hand that was truly holding onto it in the first place, but God's.

When you are going through a trial, you have a choice to keep your faith in God, or falter. If you choose to have faith, it produces patience. Because as you are waiting for a trial to end, you are already believing that it will end, because God's hand is in it, it's just a matter of time. Which in turn, produces patience. But, if you choose to doubt the whole time, then you are not believing that God will come through for you. Now this isn't to say that you won't have moments of doubt. We are all human, and we all have those moments. But, as long as you quickly take your mind off of that doubt, as soon as possible, and turn it back to God, this is faith. That no matter what your flesh says, no matter what things may look like, and no matter how you feel, you know beyond a shadow of a doubt that God will come through for you, because you know and believe that what the word says is true. And the word says that God, is always faithful.

Know therefore that the LORD your God is God; he is the faithful God, keeping his covenant of love to a thousand generations of those who love him and keep his commandments.

Deuteronomy 7:9

James 1:9-11

This isn't saying that it's bad to be rich. I believe this passage tells us something similar to this scripture below.

For where your treasure is, there your heart will be also.

Matthew 6:21

If you are chasing after the things of this world, then you are not chasing after God. Not fully anyways. You can't have both. You can't have half of God and half of the world. It doesn't work that way. God is a jealous God and He doesn't want to share you with worldly things. See also Exodus 20:5-6. This means that you

6

either want to go your own way and after what the world says should be your focus, or you can focus on God and the way He chooses for you to go. You can't make money and God your idol. You can only have one or the other. This doesn't mean that you can't be passionate about things, because you can. It's more about what you are putting first. You can't have what you are wanting sharing the spotlight with God. God should always come first. If you are working your way towards a really good job, or maybe you are passionate about art or singing, this is all great, but you need God to be first and foremost in your life. If you believe that you do put God first, ask yourself this. What are you most passionate about in life, aside from God. What are you striving towards? It could be something you want to be like a singer, or it can be buying that new home, or starting a family. Now after you finish finding out what you are hoping for, ask yourself this. If God says no to whatever you are asking, are you willing to lay it down at His feet? Are you willing to fully surrender it and leave it there? You can't say that you surrender it and then take it back either. That's not full surrender. If I give you a gift, and then a month later, I decide I wanted it, it wouldn't be very pleasing to the person I gave it to, when I come and ask for it back. How do you think God feels when we come to Him in full surrender, give Him everything we have, and then a week, month, or year later, we decide we want it back? It's like me giving you something that you have been really wanting, and then getting it for you, and then taking it back. It wouldn't be right. I get it, surrendering is hard. Just because you should surrender everything to God, doesn't mean that it's easy. That's why surrendering is a form of sacrifice. When you sacrifice something for someone, it means that you are giving up something. A lot of times it means giving up something that you really don't want to give up. When you sacrifice your own free time to spend more time with your kids, or take less hours at work to spend more time with a spouse, it's sacrificing for the benefit of someone else. But, it also benefits you as well. You get closer with your kids or your spouse by sacrificing that time that you were allocating to something else, and giving it to them. In the same sense, surrendering benefits you. God doesn't need you to surrender, He wants you to. God already has everything that He needs. He is God. He doesn't NEED anything from us. But that doesn't mean that He doesn't want things from us. His want doesn't come from anything but a place of love. He loves us and wants to help us. When we surrender, it allows Him to do this, unhindered.

This scripture tells us that the rich man will fade away in his pursuits. The rich may seem to prosper and their life may seem beautiful, but it will soon fade away like a flower of the field, and judgment day will come. You can pursue all the worldly things in life like money, fame, cars, homes, etc. But what you need to realize, is that it will fade away. There will be a day when all that you worked for will be gone. Then what will you have? But, if you store up treasures in heaven, where no moth or rust can destroy, where no thieves can steal it, and where those treasures don't fade away or get destroyed, this is better than the latter. See also Matthew 6:19-21. Why work for things that fade away? As I said, it's not wrong to work towards goals in life, but what comes first? God, or the thing that you are chasing after? When we die, nothing comes with us. If you follow treasures of this world, they will eventually come to nothing. But, if you follow Jesus, He never fades. We are alive for but a breath. Here one day and gone the next. Make sure you make your time here on earth count for something more than mere earthly things. Focus on Jesus, follow Jesus, and tell others about Jesus. One day we all have to come face to face with the One who created us. When you do, will you be happy with how you lived your life?

<u>James 1:12-14</u>

The enemy will try everything that God allows him to, in order to make you fall into temptation. As you can see, I used the words, God allows. God doesn't tempt you, as God cannot be tempted by evil, nor does He tempt anyone. But, He does allow things to happen. When God does allow something in your life, it's because it serves a purpose. Ask yourself this. Would a loving Father allow a trial just to hurt you? You don't have to have kids or even a good earthly dad in order to understand this concept. All you need, is love. Love is what drives God to allow the things that He does. Let me give you an example. If my child walks up to a hot stove, should I just leave him? Of course not! I would tell him not to touch it. When I do, depending on how young they are, they may cry for being told no. They don't understand that I am only trying to protect them from getting hurt. Am I still sad to see them upset? Of course I am! I never want to see my kid sad or cry, but sometimes, it's necessary. Did I not allow my child to touch the hot stove, just so that they could cry and be upset and sad? No, my main reason came from a place of love. You may not understand it now, but soon you will. Soon you will realize that I was only trying to protect you. Sometimes God protects us from others, and sometimes from ourselves. Sometimes He does something that we don't understand, and like the child trying to touch the hot stove, we too throw a tantrum, get upset, sad, or even depressed. It can be God telling us no, God closing a door, not hearing from Him the way that we want, the time that we want, or even a trial in your life that you just can't understand why you have to go through it. God's ways and thoughts are higher than ours. He sees what's ahead and He knows the best and most prosperous paths to take. That doesn't mean that it won't hurt, but it does mean that you can trust that God knows what He is doing.

Now let's also look at the verse that talks about being drawn and enticed by our own desires. I believe that when someone reads the bible it can mean different things for different people. Why? Because it's alive and active. God's word is always speaking. That doesn't mean that one person's interpretation is right, and the other person's interpretation is wrong. What it does mean, is that God speaks to us in different ways, at different times. It's good to weigh others interpretations, because sometimes it spreads more light on a passage. But, please be careful to pray and ask God to keep your eyes open, because some people are out to deceive others. And I tell you this, because it's important to know. Some people are false prophets, false witnesses, and false believers. You can tell them by their fruits, you can tell them by their words, their actions, etc. Sometimes they will say a lot of things that sound right, but then add something that sounds a little off, but the rest sounds right so you believe it. Be careful. This is how satan deceives you. He does it subtly and slowly. That way, you don't notice it until it's too late, and you have all this false doctrine in your mind that it's leading you down the wrong path, and now you need to remove it all. So please, be careful when reading commentaries or study bibles, no matter who they are from. Now back to what I was saying. Let's say that you are a recovering alcoholic. If you get tempted to have a drink, it is your desire to have the drink that entices you. This is why it says that *"But each one is tempted when he is drawn away by his own desires and enticed."* And who is doing the enticing? It may be that you have an alcoholic friend that tries to get you to drink, but, if you pull the curtain back, the enemy is the one in the shadows. That's why if you are in a situation like this, you should pray to God and ask if that friend should still be in your life. Sometimes in order to move forward, we need to leave things behind.

James 1:17-18

Don't be deceived into thinking that anything you have or own is from yourself or others. God gives you every good and perfect gift. Let's take a baby for example. The baby may be born from a biological moms stomach, but that doesn't mean that the baby came from her. She harbored the gift, but she didn't give the gift. The gift came from God. This is the same concept when it comes to everything else in life. If you got a good job, yes you had the interview and got the job, but God was the one who was with your mouth, and with the interviewers heart, impressing on them if they should hire you or not. We get deceived into thinking that we are doing these things on our own, but it couldn't be farther from the truth. It's God, it's always God. So before you go praising yourself or others for whatever it is you have, go to God first. He deserves your praise. I'm not saying that you shouldn't thank the person giving you the job, because you should, but remember where it truly came from. God gets the glory, no one else.

God doesn't change. He isn't one day this way and another the next. He isn't like us. We go by how we feel a lot of times. One day were in a good mood and 5 seconds later we're screaming, because something upset us. That's not how God is. He isn't a mere human being that He would act this way. Shifting and changing with the winds and waves of the sea. He is always the same. A loving, faithful Father who loves His children dearly. He is nothing short of a great Father.

He didn't make us because He had to, or because He was told to. He did it from His own free will. He did it because He loves us, more than you or I could ever imagine. He did it because although He didn't need us, He wanted us. So much in fact, that He sent His one and only Son to die for us. So don't ever question if God wants or loves you, because His actions show that He truly does.

James 1:19-20

Be quick to give a listening ear, but not so quick to speak. Giving careful thought of your words. Remember, we are ambassadors for Christ. Let your words show it. When others talk to you, do you resemble Christ? We are meant to be lights in this darkened world. When others see us, they should see Jesus. If your words or your actions don't show that, then maybe you need to reevaluate your ways. None of us are perfect. There is always something in us that needs work. That's why it's good to ask God the same thing that David did in Psalms.

Search me, O God, and know my heart;
Try me, and know my anxieties;
And see if there is any wicked way in me,
And lead me in the way everlasting.

Psalms 139:23-24

We also need to keep our emotions in check. We rule them, not the other way around. We have the authority over our feelings to say no, I'm not going to be upset today. I'm not going to be sad or down today. God gave us authority to rule over our feelings. Is it easy? Far from it! But we don't need easy, just possible.

God is slow to anger with us, even though we don't deserve it. He is patient, He is kind. Let us walk in this same manner. In a manner pleasing to God. Remember, anger is never, and will never be a fruit of the spirit, so don't let it be in yours.

James 1:21-25

The only overflow that should be coming from you, are ones that are worthy of your calling. The fruits of the Spirit.

But the fruit of the Spirit is love, joy, peace, longsuffering, kindness, goodness, faithfulness, gentleness, self-control. Against such there is no law.

Galatians 5:22-23

All anger and malice, leave at the door. All jealousy and rage, leave at the door. Anything that is considered wickedness in God's eyes, should be considered wickedness in your eyes as well, as Christ is in you, and it is no longer you who lives, but Christ in you.

Be submissive to the word. Don't look at the word, read the word, and simply walk away from it as if you never heard it. This passage reminds you not to forget who you are in Christ. Don't just read the word and then forget. The bible is not some book to be read and then forgotten, but followed, closely. It's not any book, it's not any words, but the living one. It's alive and active.

For the word of God is living and powerful, and sharper than any two-edged sword, piercing even to the division of soul and spirit, and of joints and marrow, and is a discerner of the thoughts and intents of the heart.

Hebrews 4:12

How many books can you name that you can say for certain pierce soul, spirit, joints, and marrow? I know of only one. Some books can help you, some books make you happy, some sad, but this is not the same. This goes so much deeper than that. It heals you, binds up your wounds, lets you know who you are in Christ, and how you should live as followers of Christ, among many other things. What other book can you say is God-breathed? I love how the NIV puts the scripture below.

All Scripture is God-breathed and is useful for teaching, rebuking, correcting and training in righteousness, so that the servant of God may be thoroughly equipped for every good work.

2 Timothy 3:16-17

You cannot simply find another book comparable to the bible. One that tells us how Jesus walked the earth, what is to come in the final days, what happened during the creation process, who and what God created first, how we ought to live, etc. This is invaluable information. You can't replace this. It is one of a kind, so treat it as such. Receive the word, and follow what it says, for it is able to save your soul. The one who follows the word is blessed in what he does.

Many people see completing the bible as a huge milestone. Some people may brag about it, some may feel joyful and accomplished. Don't get me wrong, it is an accomplishment and something to be joyful for. I'm not diminishing the fact that it's a great feeling to finish the bible, or that you shouldn't feel a sense of joy when you complete it, because you should. But ask yourself, how did you complete it? Did you rush through the pages, or did you spend time not just reading, but listening? Are you planning on reading it one time and then be done? If so, that's not what God intended. We are specifically told to meditate on it day and night. What about your why? Why did you complete it? Was it to get to know God, or was it to feel more "religious". Did you complete it because you love God? Because you love Him and just wanted to know Him more? The why is important, the why matters. Would you rather God watch over you and spend time with you because He has to, or because He loves you, because He wants to? As I said, the why matters. If you completed the bible, it is something to be joyful over, but, remember your why.

Remember, don't just know the word, don't just memorize the word, but live out the word.

James 1:26-27

Humans use something called a bridle on a horse.

A bridle helps give direction to a horse, ultimately, controlling it. There are 3 pieces to a bridle. One for the mouth, one for the head, and one for the reins. The one for the mouth is called a bit. The bit goes over/on top of the horses tongue. So in the same sense, we should be controlling our tongues with his same bit. Using the reigns to tell it what to say and what not to say. In James 3 it tells us this.

For every kind of beast and bird, of reptile and creature of the sea, is tamed and has been tamed by mankind. But no man can tame the tongue. It is an unruly evil, full of deadly poison. With it we bless our God and Father, and with it we curse men, who have been made in the similitude of God. Out of the same mouth proceed blessing and cursing. My brethren, these things ought not to be so. Does a spring send forth fresh water and bitter from the same opening? Can a fig tree, my brethren, bear olives, or a grapevine bear figs? Thus no spring yields both salt water and fresh.

James 3:7-12

So here we can see, that taming the tongue is not a simple thing. It's difficult. We need to apply pressure to our tongue with the reigns, guiding it where to go. You will get resistance, as the tongue according to this scripture, cannot be tamed. However, we should still be trying to. Why? Because this is what we are told to do. To control it. Just like a horse, the more you work at it and train it, the more it listens.

What we are called to do, is love. Visiting widows and orphans, and simply, loving others. This is what is acceptable in God's eyes. We see clearly about this kind of love in 1 Corinthians 13. Please take some time to read it if you don't know it or remember it.

Keep yourself separate from the world. If God were to visit you today, what would He see? Would He see the world, or Himself? Remember, God sees what you do in every moment of everyday. And we also know that the return of Jesus will come like a thief in the night, so be prepared. Be ready for His return so that when you stand before Him, you will know that you tried your absolute best to please Him.

James 2:1-13

God does not judge by mere appearances, so why do you? If someone has tattoos, is homeless, looks unrelatable, looks mean, looks like they are a bad person, etc, why do you judge by mere appearances? Just because they look mean, doesn't mean they are. Just because someone looks like a bad person, doesn't mean that they are. Let me ask you something, if a man covered in tattoos sits next to you in church, would you feel uncomfortable? What about a man well groomed and in fancy clothes? We are not to show partiality to others. Meaning that we should not be favoring one over the other. Does God love one of us more than the other? Does God only show his love to the well groomed and rich? We should also do as God would do. God looks at the heart.

But the LORD said to Samuel, "Do not consider his appearance or his height, for I have rejected him. The LORD does not look at the things people look at. People look at the outward appearance, but the LORD looks at the heart."

1 Samuel 16:7

The fact is, that man covered in tattoos may have a beautiful heart and the rich well groomed man sitting next to you may be a proud man that only cares about himself. We forget at times, that the way someone looks on the outside, doesn't show the true nature of the person on the inside. People need to know that they are loved, regardless of their appearance, financial status, social status, etc. Somewhere along the way, as a society, we have been losing the main ingredient of who God calls us to be. That main ingredient is love.

And now abide faith, hope, love, these three; but the greatest of these is love.

1 Corinthians 13:13

We are to love our neighbors as ourselves. You may ask, who is my neighbor? Here is your answer.

But he, wanting to justify himself, said to Jesus, "And who is my neighbor?"

Then Jesus answered and said: "A certain man went down from Jerusalem to Jericho, and fell among thieves, who stripped him of his clothing, wounded him, and departed, leaving him half dead. Now by chance a certain priest came down that road. And when he saw him, he passed by on the other side. Likewise a Levite, when he arrived at the place, came and looked, and passed by on the other side. But a certain Samaritan, as he journeyed, came where he was. And when he saw him, he had compassion. So he went to him and bandaged his wounds, pouring on oil and wine; and he set him on his own animal, brought him to an inn, and took care of him. On the next day, when he departed, he took out two denarii, gave them to the innkeeper, and said to him, 'Take care of him; and whatever more you spend, when I come again, I will repay you.' So which of these three do you think was neighbor to him who fell among the thieves?"

And he said, "He who showed mercy on him."

Then Jesus said to him, "Go and do likewise."

Luke 10:29-37

A neighbor is not just someone who lives next to you. We are called to love everyone. Even your enemies. We see this in Matthew.

You have heard that it was said, 'You shall love your neighbor and hate your enemy.' But I say to you, love your enemies, bless those who curse you, do good to those who hate you, and pray for those who spitefully use you and persecute you

Matthew 5:43-44

18

I understand that it can be difficult to love someone who uses you, treats you unfairly, makes fun of you, or makes you feel unwanted. As hard as it can be, this is what we are called to do. Jesus was treated very unfairly. Yet he never retaliated and used His power to hurt others. He came to save the world, remember. This reminds me of a scripture in 1 Peter.

Wives, likewise, be submissive to your own husbands, that even if some do not obey the word, they, without a word, may be won by the conduct of their wives

1 Peter 3:1

This shows you that your conduct towards others and the way that you treat them, can bring them to God, even if they don't know Him. Just as insects are drawn to the light, so are people. They are drawn to the light within us, Jesus Christ. We are the lights of the world and called to be as such. So let your light shine before men, glorifying your Father in heaven.

The same God who told us to love our neighbor as ourselves, is the same God who gave the 10 commandments. If you break one law, you break them all. Therefore, if you show favoritism to anyone, you are committing sin. Likewise, if you break any of the words and rules that are in God's word, you are also committing sin. Committing sin is committing sin, no matter the degree of it, it is still sin. One day, we will be judged for our words and actions, therefore, speak and do as God calls you to. Knowing that one day, you will be face to face with the One who created you and the law.

Show compassion towards one another, forgiving one another, just as Christ has forgiven you. If you show no compassion or forgiveness towards others, it will also be shown to you likewise.

For what measure you give to others, it will be given to you. See also Luke 6:38.

Remember, mercy triumphs over judgment.

James 2:14-26

As Christians, we know that faith is essential in our walk with God. I have noticed that too often, we forget to include what comes with faith. Faith without works is dead. If you tell me that you saw someone in need and hungry, and you prayed for them, I can reply with I too, saw someone in need and hungry, and I prayed with them and gave them bread. Show me your faith without works, and I will show you my faith, by my works. Your faith says that you believe in God. Demons believe the same, and they shudder. Believing in God, and allowing your actions to show that you believe in God, go hand in hand. You can't have one without the other. If you say that you believe in God and you read the word, yet every day you go party, drink, use foul language, walk the wide path, go against God's word, etc, then your mouth says faith, but your actions show otherwise. Ask yourself this question. When others look at you, what do they see? Do they see Jesus, or do they see a worldly influence, a thief, a potty mouth, etc? What do they see? No one is perfect and we all have things that we need to work on. We are imperfect people and until Jesus comes to get us, this is how it will be. However, that doesn't mean that we need to blend in with the world. In fact, we need to stand out. How do you think the lost get found? It's not by seeing a worldly person who does things that they shouldn't. It's by being different. It's by standing out from the crowd. It's by going your own way when the world says no. It's by going the opposite way that the crowd goes, and being bold enough and courageous enough to do it. Because what you believe in, you believe in so much, that you don't care what anyone thinks. That's how you truly draw people in. Not by blending in with the world, but by standing out. So I urge you, stand out. Come out from among them and be separate. We are not of the world, but foreigners of this world. We were never meant to be like the world, but to be like Jesus. And when we are like Jesus, we stand out. Many people sought after Jesus to kill Him. Why? Because He stood out. He was different. He didn't cave in to the world, to it's beliefs, and to it's nature. They wanted Jesus to go by their beliefs, because they were too stubborn to change their own. They were blinded by this world and they sought to remove anyone who wasn't blind with them. Therefore, Jesus suffered, and so do we. Standing out may not be easy, but it is necessary. How can you be a light in a darkened world, when you are moving along the path of darkness? If I am moving along the path of darkness, how can anyone see Jesus's light? But, if I move away from that darkness, my light gets brighter, because I am no longer moving in the direction of darkness. I moved from the wide path to the narrow path, I am standing out. Which would you notice more? Someone in regular every day clothes, or someone with a sweater that lights up, even in darkness? Yes, you may face adversity, yes, you may even be made fun of, or questioned about your beliefs, but so was Jesus, and He overcame this world. Let your light shine like Jesus intended it to shine. Come out, be separate.

When I read the part about Abraham and Isaac, it reminded me of a scripture in Matthew.

"But what do you think? A man had two sons, and he came to the first and said, 'Son, go, work today in my vineyard.' He answered and said, 'I will not,' but afterward he regretted it and went. Then he came to the second and said likewise. And he

answered and said, 'I go, sir,' but he did not go. Which of the two did the will of his father?"

They said to Him, "The first."

Jesus said to them, "Assuredly, I say to you that tax collectors and harlots enter the kingdom of God before you. For John came to you in the way of righteousness, and you did not believe him; but tax collectors and harlots believed him; and when you saw it, you did not afterward relent and believe him.

Matthew 21:28-32

As you can see, our actions matter. You can tell God that you will do as He says all day until you are blue in the face, but none of it means anything, unless you actually do it. Saying you will do something, but not doing it, doesn't please God. It takes action. Are you actually doing what God is asking you to do, or are you just saying you will do as He wants? Are you only doing the things that fit what you want, or are you doing all the things that He asks of you?

Your faith, works together with your works. You are not justified by faith alone. Remember that.

When one dies, their spirit leaves their body. The body then decays, because the spirit has left the body. The body without the spirit, is dead. Faith, without works, is also dead. You need faith, but you also need works for the faith to be active, to be alive, and to work the way that God had intended for it to work, for the kingdom of God.

To see more examples of faith working with action, please read Hebrews 11

James 3:1

The ones who teach the word, are under stricter judgment. I look at it like this. Let's say that I am reading the word. I come across a passage that I don't understand, so I either grab something online that sounds right, or I write something, not knowing if it's correct, because I am confused on the subject. If it's wrong, I am teaching myself false doctrine. However, if I then share that with others, I am then teaching them false doctrine. It is one thing to teach yourself something against God's word, which yes is still wrong, but it's completely another thing to teach others that same false doctrine. If I teach someone God's word, I am now accountable for the words that I teach. The words that I say, as well as the ones that I don't say. Take a Pastor for example. Let's say that a pastor has a congregation of 50. That would be 50 people that are learning false doctrine, who then may spread it to their kids, friends, spouse, etc. Then those people spread it to others, and so on and so forth. We need to be careful with the words we use. Especially when teaching others. I once heard someone teaching a congregation of hundreds false doctrine. He was falsely telling the congregation never to ask God about His will. He said it's not God's will, it's your will. He of course, was what we call a false prophet, but that's another story. My point is, be careful with what you hear. Guard your hearts and your minds. Also be careful with what you speak, and with what you share. There is tons of false information going around. Some being deliberately done, and some accidental. One I can also think of is a rumor about an eagle and how in order to survive it must pluck it's feathers, talons, and beak, to live past 30 or 40.

It's completely false information. However, if you type on a search bar, eagle plucking it's feathers, it's everywhere. Sometimes when something spreads like a wildfire, we assume it's true. This couldn't be farther from the truth. How did this rumor about the eagle spread so far and so wide? Because someone taught it to someone, and they taught it to someone else, and so on and so forth. This is why if you are teaching or sharing anything with anyone, be careful that you check your facts before spreading it. Because as you can see, it can spread. It can have a much farther reach than you could ever imagine.

James 3:2

None of us are exempt from stumbling. We all stumble at one point or another. If you have never stumbled, then you are perfect, and we all know that there was only one man who ever walk this earth that was perfect. His name is Jesus. There never was, is, or will be anyone like Him.

It is not shameful to say that you have stumbled, it is honest. As a society we are taught to keep our feelings in. We are taught that you don't want someone to think you're crazy, unstable, or have any issues. So, we need to look perfect on the outside, which only makes us depressed, sad, and screaming on the inside. Even in church we do it. We say how are you, only to hear that they are great or fine. I'm sure you do it as well, as have I. But what would happen if someone actually admitted to not being fine? Why do you think we shy away from our feelings? Is it fear of what others may think, fear of being rejected, or fear of judgment? What about you? If someone came up to you and you said how are you, and they said not good, how would you respond? Would you say I'm so sorry to hear that, I'll keep you in my prayers, or would you ask them if they would like to talk about it? Would you tell them that you would love to listen, if they are willing to share? Remember, *If one of you says to them, "Go in peace; keep warm and well fed," but does nothing about their physical needs, what good is it?*

We have created these domes of steel around us. We are so afraid to let anyone in. We have a tendency to hide our feelings. Fear of judgment or what someone may say about us, to us, or behind our backs. I recall Paul spreading the gospel, as well as sharing the things that he has been through, his hardships that he faced. Do we judge him for them, or do they give us strength? Hearing that others stumble just as we do, gives us hope, courage to fight another day, and strength to keep going. Sometimes sharing our story provides strength to someone who just needed to hear that someone else is going through difficulty, or has been through difficulty, and is still fighting, still believing, still hopeful, and still full of faith. It encourages us more than just saying I'm good or I'm fine all the time. God never made us to be solitary creatures. We are meant to help each other, love each other, and need each other. It could be a stranger passing in the store, who really needed someone to just notice them. Someone to hear them when their voice feels so unheard. It could be sharing a piece of your life with someone who just needs to hear that everything will be OK, because you have seen a God who loves, a God who heals, a God who is faithful, and a God who is with you always.

Remember, it's OK to stumble, and it's OK to need help sometimes. We are imperfect people living in an imperfect world, and we all need a little encouragement at times, as do I. No one is exempt from this.

James 3:3-12

A rudder to a ship is small in comparison to the actual ship. Yet even though it is small, it can boast great things. If a rudder could talk, I am sure that it would boast great things, considering it controls an entire ship. Your tongue also, is a small part, yet it boasts many things. With the same tongue we bless people and pray to God, and with it we also curse others, demean others, and use God's name in vain. This my friends, should not be so. The tongue can be a cruel weapon, used to tear someone down, make them feel useless, alone, and unwanted. But, if we use that same tongue for good, we can use that same weapon that was once being used for darkness, and use it as a weapon of light instead. We can bring someone up, make them feel loved, never alone, and wanted. We alone choose whether or not we have a tight rein on our tongue. One cannot say, "I just can't control what I say", because as one can train a horse with a bridle, we too can train our tongues, but it takes persistence, practice, restraint, and self-control. Just as training a horse cannot be done in a day, neither can training our tongue. Even if a horse is fully trained and remembers it's training, it is still good to give occasional reminders of that training. We too need reminders that we should be using our tongue for good, not for evil, lest we let our surroundings or hardships make us forget who we are in Christ. We all have to make a choice. We can act as if the bit were in our mouth, and we are holding the reigns, or, we can choose to let it run free, and allow it to praise God and curse others all the same. As a rudder controls the ship, the tongue can also control us. However, if you look closely at a ship, you can then realize that the one who actually controls the ship, is us. We turn the rudder where we want it to go. We tell the rudder to go right, to go left, or to stay still. We control the rudder. If the rudder were to control itself, we would never get to where we are wanting to go, and we may possibly even end up on the bottom of an ocean somewhere. Harsh, but true. In the same sense, we have a tongue, which can control where we go in life, the things we say, the things we don't say. However, we are the one that is truly steering the ship. The tongue may be able to say as it pleases, but we have to give it the okay. Just because it has the ability to move, doesn't mean that it can or should move on it's own. We give the okay for that to happen. We send the signal to our tongue, just as we send the signal to the rudder. We went over the fact that if a rudder was in control, we may end up in the bottom of the ocean. Your tongue can do likewise. You can hurt those you love, make someone feel bad about themselves, hurt God's feelings, hurt your own feelings, etc. You choose whether you use it for good, or for evil. Remember, steer your tongue, don't let it steer you.

Our tongue is compared to a fire. It only takes a spark, to start a forest fire. One word, can start a war. One word can cause resentment, divorce, and even suicide. One word is all it takes to start a fire. It starts with one word. One that may seem so

27

insignificant at the time, but that spark spreads like a forest fire, consuming everything in it's path. One person calling someone fat, ugly, stupid, etc. One word is so powerful. We may not realize it at the time, but that one word can cause hurt, pain, resentment, and tears. One that someone may carry with them their whole life. We need to learn to tame our tongues. I believe that not all, but a lot of depression, wars, shootings, etc., come from just a few words, and can be prevented by withholding those few words. It takes only one person to make someone feel so unloved, but only one person to show them how much they are loved. Choose the latter.

James 3:13-18

If you are wise and understanding, then you will show this by your actions, by the way that you behave, and by being submissive to wisdom. Wisdom is your friend. Wisdom will guide you, and all her ways are peace. She is more precious than rubies and all things that you may desire, can not compare to her. See also Proverbs 3:14-18. Wisdom involves thinking ahead, seeing how your actions will affect things down the road, whether it's tomorrow or a year from now. It's making sure that your decision will have the desired affect, one that pleases God. Being wise is making unnecessary quick decisions. There are a lot of ways that wisdom can help you. Whether it's applying wisdom to scriptures, not making assumptions of other people or situations, having good judgment, discernment, etc. This is good wisdom. This is attaining wisdom the correct way, through God. Through what pleases Him. There is good wisdom, wise wisdom, but, there is also worldly wisdom. Wanting what others want, using wisdom to attain worldly things, looking after your own hearts and the desires of this world, etc. The wisdom of this world goes against scripture, ultimately, going against God. You can get distracted by the wants in this life, but the wants in this life, are but a breath. They are temporary. While they may give you a temporary satisfaction, it wont last. If you are desiring money, it won't last. Eventually you will pass away and that money that you spent your whole life desiring and keeping your eyes on, is now gone. Then, you have to face God and answer why you sought money, houses, cars, etc, instead of Him. I am not saying that wanting to be well off or wanting a home is a bad thing. These are good things to strive fore. Wanting to better your family financially etc. What is bad though, is if that's all you care about. What is bad, is if you want the money, the cars, the dream job, the fame, more than you want God. God should always be in the front. He shouldn't even be in the same field as the rest. When you look to God, all you should see is God, nothing else. The money, fame, cars, etc, should all be so much lower, that you can't even see them. They are so much lower that if God says no, you are OK with it, because you desire Him more. You desire to please Him more. You love Him, more.

Godly wisdom is pure, has good motives, is gentle, seeking others before themselves, God before things of this world. Willing to stop when God says stop, to go when He says go, to wait when He says wait. Wisdom shows no favor, and doesn't let feelings get in the way of what you believe in. Wisdom that is from above and pure and always does what's right in God's eyes, not the world's eyes. Wisdom produces good fruit, and shows mercy to all. God shows mercy to us time and time again, we should be doing the same. It is sown in peace, because all of wisdom's paths are peace. Wisdom is precious, wisdom is vital. God used wisdom to found the earth, by understanding He established the heavens. See also Proverbs 3:19-20.

Remember, as you are getting wisdom, in all your getting, get understanding.

Wisdom is the principal thing;
Therefore get wisdom.
And in all your getting, get understanding.

Proverbs 4:7

James 4:1

I did some research on the causes of different wars that have happened. Do you know what I found? Wars began initially from wants of this world. Wanting to separate and be your own country, wanting more land, more power, more control, etc. The wars may have escalated to other things such as assassinations, etc, but the initial reason remains the same. Greed, envy, worldly desires, etc. We fight, we war, we quarrel. 2 Timothy 2:23-26 tells us to do just the opposite. To avoid foolish and ignorant disputes, knowing that they generate strife. Meaning that it only causes conflict. Unnecessary conflict. A servant of the Lord must not quarrel, but be gentle to all. We must be patient. We must look out for one another. God did not put us on this earth to fight, but to love. Remember, Jesus didn't come to this world to condemn it, but to save it.

James 4:2-3

You do things that are of this world, to get the things of this world. People steal, murder, and lie. Going against God's commandments, just to gain the temporary pleasures of this world. As we see in Romans 7:9-25, sin is alive in all of us. We all wage war against sin everyday. Our spirit and our flesh clash. We want to do good, but our flesh wages war against the good that tries to be done. And until we reach heavens gates, until we are free from this fleshly body, and until satan gets thrown into the fire pit where he belongs, this is what we have to deal with. While we are on this earth, this is what we have to do. We have to fight, everyday. We have to fight to do what's right. We have to command that our flesh stays in check, and that our spirit rules the flesh. Everyday we have to submit and surrender to the Holy Spirit. Everyday. You can say I surrender and that be that. It has to be a daily sacrifice to surrender your life, your heart, your mind, your soul, your spirit, your flesh, your will, your life. Daily. Everyday, every moment, and every second, you have to surrender.

As a society, we want things now. We want an order same day, we want the solution now, and when we don't get it we throw a fit. We feel entitled to know everything when we want to know it. Everyone has done this, myself included. You want a home, and you want it now. You want a job, and you want it now. We are being programmed to want things fast, but friends, this is not how God works. Look at how long Jesus waited for His ministry to start, look at how long God waited for redemption of mankind, look at how long God is still waiting to be with all those He loves. He is still waiting to this day. He is waiting for the day that He makes everything new again. God doesn't do instant, although yes, at times He does, but a lot of the times, we are called to wait. Wait for an answer, wait for that job, that healing, that child to come home, that addiction to break, that anxiety to break, etc. Everything takes time. And as we see in Ecclesiastes, God does make all things beautiful, but it's in His time. No one knows what God does from the beginning to the end, and so we couldn't possibly know what's up ahead. So the times where it looks like God isn't working, He really is. Why? Because you can't see what He does from beginning to end. His knowledge and His wisdom and His understanding, is so vast, so infinite, that our finite minds couldn't possibly comprehend all that He has done, or will do in our lives. That's why it's so important to follow what scriptures say when it tells us not to lean on our own understanding. Why? Because our understanding is so small. So minuscule compared to our Father's. You couldn't possibly comprehend all that He has been working on in your life. We aren't meant to know or understand everything, we are meant to trust. To trust that God knows what He is doing, to trust that He knows best. That's why in this passage in James says

Yet you do not have because you do not ask. You ask and do not receive, because you ask amiss, that you may spend it on your pleasures.
James 4:2-3

It's saying that you don't ask, but when you do ask, you ask with wrong motives. You do it for your own pleasures, your own

32

desires, and not God's. And, even if you are asking because you want to truly know God's will, you need to trust that He knows best. This means that when He says no, you trust that He knows best. Also, no doesn't mean no forever, although it can, but it can also mean no for right now. Maybe it's just not time yet, maybe you aren't ready yet, or maybe the circumstances aren't right yet. It can even be because others are not ready yet. God is perfect, and He knows exactly what you will need when you need it, and that means that He doesn't want to move you until its His perfect timing. Until your ready, others are ready, your situation, and your circumstances are ready. What do you do while you wait? Pray, get closer to God, read, and get ready. Prepare yourself to be used however He sees fit. There is a saying that God doesn't call the equipped, He equips the called. While yes, I do believe this, I also believe that we do play a part. If God calls you, but you refuse to read His word, pray, and spend time getting to know Him, then you are not doing your part. While we wait, we are not supposed to sit dormant. We are supposed to get to know Him more. Not off of the basis that we will get rewarded for it, but just because we love Him and want to spend time with Him. When you come to His word, or come to Him in prayer, don't make it all about you. Thank Him for His goodness, thank Him for what He has given you. When you read, do it off of the basis of just wanting to know Him more. To know who your Creator is, who the Potter is. As you read His word, you will start to align with His will, becoming more and more like Jesus everyday that you spend time with Him. Focus on Him, and everything else will fall into place. This reminds me of a scripture in Luke. When Martha was so worried about all of the tasks that needed to be done, she came to Jesus asking Him to tell her sister to help. Look at Jesus's response.

But Martha was distracted with much serving, and she approached Him and said, "Lord, do You not care that my sister has left me to serve alone? Therefore tell her to help me."

And Jesus answered and said to her, "Martha, Martha, you are worried and troubled about many things. But one thing is needed, and Mary has chosen that good part, which will not be taken away from her."

Luke 10:40-42

Where is your main focus? Is it on the many worries of this life, or is it where it needs to be, on Jesus?

Fill your name in the blanks. _____, _____, you are worried and troubled about many things. But one thing is needed.

Remember to keep your eyes on Jesus, and the rest will fall into place, in God's timing.

James 4:4

You can not be friends with this world and God at the same time. They both clash. They both desire different things. You can't please both, and you can't want both. It's one or the other. The world often goes one way, as God goes the other. You will be torn in two. It's not feasible to go in two opposite directions. It's like saying that you can walk left and right at the same time. It's not capable of being done, and eventually, you will have to choose.

You will have to make the choice to follow worldly desires, or God's. But I can tell you that God's way is so much better. It may be harder, but still better. Jesus didn't have an easy road when He walked this earth, and we are called to do the same. To take up our cross and follow Him, even through difficulty. Even in rain, snow, and thunderstorms, we are to follow. But just as the eye of the storm is calm, you can also have the storm around you, and not in you. Everything in your life can be going so wrong. Pieces of your life are flying everywhere, and pain is everywhere you look, but, just because the chaos is around you, just because the storms are around you, doesn't mean that they have to be in you. Why? Because you are grounded in more than mere worldly chaos. You are not built on sand, but on the Rock. I love the verse that says,

From the end of the earth I will cry to You,
When my heart is overwhelmed;
Lead me to the rock that is higher than I.

Psalms 61:2

You can be in pain, yet still focused. You can be sick, hurting, and unsure of what's ahead, while still keeping focus on the One who does know what's up ahead. Because He is your rock, your shelter, and your firm foundation. So yes, you can choose to be friends with the world, but the world is mere sand. It blows away at the sound of trials, hardships, and life. Building your life on sand, won't last. Maybe, for a while it may seem like it, but little by little, it will slowly strip away, until you come to the end of yourself, and you hopefully realize that you need a sturdier foundation. Jesus Christ Himself. You can't get a stronger foundation anywhere else. It can't be found anywhere else, made anywhere else, or thought of anywhere else. Jesus Christ is the only way. And that my friend, is the truth.

James 4:6

When pride comes, then comes shame;
But with the humble is wisdom.

Proverbs 11:2

By pride comes nothing but strife,
But with the well-advised is wisdom.

Proverbs 13:10

Pride goes before destruction,
And a haughty spirit before a fall.

Proverbs 16:18

Pride destroys people. Pride says that I did this on my own, everything I own is mine, my accomplishments brought me here, etc. Don't you know, oh foolish one, that you have only what God has allowed you to have? Your home is not your own, your body, is not even your own. Only One gives life, and only One allows that life to be taken away. Only One. That One is God. God sees all, knows all, and is everywhere. He allows things to be set in motion, He allows you to get that job, He allows you to get fired from that job, only God allows any of it. Pride is a terrible thing. If you remove the Creator, from the created, you have a useless creation. Let me explain. If I create a pot, and that pot tells me, I don't need you, I can do it on my own. How useless that pot has become. It needs the hands that made it, to be of any good use.

Without it's creator, its futile, meaning pointless. We too, need our Creator. We need God to be of any use. We need His guidance, His plans, and His will. God's hand is in the life of everyone, even in those who don't know it or believe it. God's hand is on the wicked and the righteous. God doesn't leave anything to mere chance. It's all in His hands. The whole world is in His hands. For someone to think that anything they have done, or anything that they have, is given by their own two hands, is false information, and dangerous. As we see in the above verse, *Pride goes before destruction, And a haughty spirit before a fall.*

Be careful where you step. Don't let pride be your downfall. Remember, all that you have, you were blessed with by God. You may have had a part in it, but it didn't come from you. Let's say that I gather rock, water, and minerals, and I make clay. I then take the clay and make a cup to drink out of. I spend time shaping it, molding it, and curing it. I paint it and make it look beautiful. Can that cup tell me that it had anything to do with making itself what it is? It played a part yes, because it was there, but it didn't have any part in anything I did. I made it from my own will, with my own hands, and with my own time, effort, and love. Now imagine if I even spoke into existence the minerals that I used to make the clay. How could it take credit for anything at that point?

Remember, everything you have, everything you own, and everything that you love, is a gift from God, never from your own hands. As it is said,

Every good gift and every perfect gift is from above, and comes down from the Father of lights, with whom there is no variation or shadow of turning.

James 1:17

James 4:7

This is a fact. It is not merely saying that if you resist the devil, <u>maybe</u> he will flee. We need to stand strong and firm in what this scripture truly means. To see this, let's also take a look at Luke 10:19.

Behold, I give you the authority to trample on serpents and scorpions, and over all the power of the enemy, and nothing shall by any means hurt you.

God didn't leave us defenseless. God gave us all the power that we needed, to defeat the enemy and his lies. So many people take this as less than what it is. It truly means that you can overcome the enemy. We are meant to conquer. We are more than conquerors.

Yet in all these things we are more than conquerors through Him who loved us.

Romans 8:37

This verse in Romans was written right after this verse below.

Who shall separate us from the love of Christ? Shall tribulation, or distress, or persecution, or famine, or nakedness, or peril, or sword? As it is written:

"For Your sake we are killed all day long;
We are accounted as sheep for the slaughter."

Romans 8:35-36

You could be in the deepest, darkest pit of your life right now, but still, you can conquer it. Conquering something, doesn't mean that you are out of whatever trial that you are in. What it means is that you don't let whats going on around you, affect who you are in you. It means that you rise above it. Why? Because God says we can. Because God gave us the power to do so. That power is not from ourselves, but from the Lord. That power dwells within us.

You are of God, little children, and have overcome them, because He who is in you is greater than he who is in the world.

1 John 4:4

We are children of the Most High. The One living within us, is greater than anything that has, is, or ever will come against us. We can overcome anything in this world. The only issue is, the devil doesn't want us to know that we can overcome the world. The enemy tries to blind us into thinking that we can't handle the situations around us, that we are too weak, too frail. But the truth of the matter is, we are strong enough to handle all of it, because we are not defenseless, and we are not alone. If you don't believe in Jesus, then yes, you don't have a leg to stand on, but if you do believe in Jesus's death and resurrection, and you love God, then what are you so afraid of? It's the enemy that tries so hard to make us feel like we are defenseless. Do you know why? Because he knows that the second we get a grip on who we truly are in Christ, that's the moment that the enemy loses his grip on us. You see, he wants us down. Why would anyone want someone else to come to the knowledge that they can destroy them? So what does he do? he is deceitful, he is the father of lies, and a murderer from the beginning. he tries to push you so far down, that you think that you have been defeated, but it couldn't be farther from the truth. The devil wants you to believe these lies, because that's how he keeps you right where he wants you. Depressed, sad, anxious, scared, fearful, feeling useless, and alone. But remember, he is a liar. Meaning that all these things are so far from the truth. This is why we are told to resist him. You have to do your part. You have to submit to God, and resist the devil. Resist him and he will flee from you. Not might, maybe, or kind of, but he will flee from you. It's a fact. Stand firm on it. Tell him no. Get behind me satan, you have to flee in the name of Jesus Christ, be gone!! Resist him, and he will flee.

James 4:8

Draw near to God, and He will draw near to you. God longs to be near you. God loves you more than you could ever imagine. I have seen His love, I have felt His love. Not only for me, but for others as well. I have seen Him work in beautiful ways in my life, as well as the lives of those around me.

Not all times, but sometimes, when we feel like we are waiting on God, He is the One that is waiting on us. Waiting on us to put our phones down and notice Him, waiting on us to skip out on a TV show just to spend time with Him, pray to Him, praise Him, and love Him. He is waiting on us. The devil tries to make us feel as if we have no time, or that we can't fit it into our schedule, to spend a few minutes with the Lord. How could you be too busy to spend time with the One who created you. Not only did He make you, but He watches over you 24/7. I'm sure that you can find at least 15 minutes in your day to spend a little time with the

One who loves you so much, that He died for you. All the pain that He suffered, was for you. It was so that He can give you life and redemption. He didn't do it for selfish gain, He did it for love. He did it because of His love for you. He did all that for you, and although you could never repay Him, can't you find some time in your busy day, for the one who gave you life? Draw near to God, and He will draw near to you.

James 4:8-10

Repent of your sins, ask God to purify your heart, and ask Him to help you be firm in your ways. Not double-minded and doubtful, but firm in all of your ways. We must always remember that we may plan our steps, but it is God who establishes them.

There is nothing wrong with admitting that you struggle. We all struggle. It takes humility to admit that you are struggling. It takes a humble heart to say, I need help. Let's say that I am swept away into the ocean by a strong current. I am struggling to stay above water. A man comes and sees my struggle and asks me if he should get a lifeguard to help. I reply with, "I don't need help, God will save me". As I am starting to get weary, I sink farther down and further out, and as I am starting to sink, a woman comes by. She asks me if I need help. I tell her no. Again, I am waiting on God to save me. I am now so far out into the ocean, that the shoreline is but a speck. I am now only using 1 arm and 1 leg to try and stay above water, because I'm too weary. I've ingested so much water and my head barely stays up at this point. A boat comes by. The people on the boat then throw me a life boat and tell me to grab on, they will pull me in. I then tell them no. I'm waiting on God to save me. They insist, but I insist more. Leave me be I say. God will save me. I refuse to grab the life boat. Eventually, after much quarreling, they leave. They tried to save my life, but I didn't want their help. I wanted God's. God would be the one to save me. I then drown. Tell me, was God not in those people that were trying to help me? Does God not send us to be His hands and feet? If I refuse the help that God is sending me, am I not refusing God Himself? God uses others to help. We see this all throughout the bible. Aaron helped Moses, the good Samaritan helped the wounded man, Jonah was sent to Ninevah to help the Ninevites, Ananias was sent to help Paul receive his sight, etc. All of these people were the ones sent to help, but it was God that worked in and through them. They were the middle-man so to speak. You see, we may be sent to do something for the Lord, but we must always remember that it is the work of God, not ourselves. The glory always goes to God. It is our duty to fulfill the things that He asks of us, but we give Him all the glory and praise, not ourselves. Why? Because we haven't done anything but what we were told to do. We obeyed Him, and so we are the hands and feet, but God is the miracle worker. It is God who does the work in us and through us, through Christ Jesus. Again, He gets the glory, not us. This reminds me of something that Jesus said in Luke.

Does he thank that servant because he did the things that were commanded him? I think not. So likewise you, when you have done all those things which you are commanded, say, 'We are unprofitable servants. We have done what was our duty to do.'

Luke 17:9-10

Remember, when God sends someone your way to help, it's OK to say that you need it. Don't get stuck in the middle of life's trials, and allow the waves to pull you under, because your too prideful to admit that you need help. If you find yourself in the middle of a struggle, remember the story about the ocean and how God did send help, but your eyes have to be open to that help. Don't be blinded by your pride. Don't be prideful, but be humble. God lifts the humble and resists the proud. Remember this verse in James 4:10 where it says,

Humble yourselves in the sight of the Lord, and He will lift you up.

And also James 4:6 where it says,

But He gives more grace. Therefore He says:
"God resists the proud,
But gives grace to the humble."

Sometimes God's help comes in the form of another person. Pray to God and ask Him to keep your eyes open and your ears willing to listen to the Holy Spirit, and to reveal to you any areas where He is trying to help you through someone else.

And remember, if you are the one doing the helping, it is always God who gets the glory, never ourselves. We are but the vessel that He chose to use in one of His magnificent plans. Thank Him for allowing you to be used, and give Him the glory, always.

<u>James 4:11-12</u>

This reminds me of a scripture in Matthew.

"Judge not, that you be not judged. For with what judgment you judge, you will be judged; and with the measure you use, it will be measured back to you. And why do you look at the speck in your brother's eye, but do not consider the plank in your own eye? Or how can you say to your brother, 'Let me remove the speck from your eye'; and look, a plank is in your own eye? Hypocrite! First remove the plank from your own eye, and then you will see clearly to remove the speck from your brother's eye.

Matthew 7:1-5

You get so busy judging others, that you don't realize that you are a sinner as well. We are all sinners. Deserving of death. Yet Jesus, in His beautiful love and mercy, died for that same sin. He took the punishment that was meant for us. He died, what was our death. What greater love, than to lay down your life for your friends, and we, are His friends. God forgave you of sins that were punishable of death, so why then, do you judge others with a harsh judgment that you too deserved, but were forgiven?

Therefore the kingdom of heaven is like a certain king who wanted to settle accounts with his servants. And when he had begun to settle accounts, one was brought to him who owed him ten thousand talents. But as he was not able to pay, his master commanded that he be sold, with his wife and children and all that he had, and that payment be made. The servant therefore fell down before him, saying, 'Master, have patience with me, and I will pay you all.' Then the master of that servant was moved with compassion, released him, and forgave him the debt.

"But that servant went out and found one of his fellow servants who owed him a hundred denarii; and he laid hands on him and took him by the throat, saying, 'Pay me what you owe!' So his fellow servant fell down at his feet and begged him, saying, 'Have patience with me, and I will pay you all.' And he would not, but went and threw him into prison till he should pay the debt. So when his fellow servants saw what had been done, they were very grieved, and came and told their master all that had been done. Then his master, after he had called him, said to him, 'You wicked servant! I forgave you all that debt because you begged me. Should you not also have had compassion on your fellow servant, just as I had pity on you?' And his master was angry, and delivered him to the torturers until he should pay all that was due to him.

"So My heavenly Father also will do to you if each of you, from his heart, does not forgive his brother his trespasses."

Matthew 18:23-35

You, who were forgiven of your trespasses, should forgive those who trespass against you. We all owed a huge debt, one that we could not afford. One punishable of death. Yet, we were shown mercy. For those who believe in Jesus Christ, in His death and resurrection, we were shown forgiveness. We were shown love.

If you are judging one another, remember, with the same measure that you use, it will be measured back to you. As God tells us, He desires mercy, not sacrifice.

James 4:13-15

We are but a breath on this earth. We are here one day, and we are gone the next. Tragedies happen, and sometimes in an instant, we are gone. We are clearly told in Matthew not to *worry about tomorrow, for tomorrow will worry about its own things. Sufficient for the day is its own trouble.* You have no clue where you will be tomorrow, let alone a year from now. You can say next year I will make more money, next year I will buy my own home, or next year, we will plan a vacation. However, it's all just words that may or may not come true. Think about it, can you really be certain that tomorrow or next year, you will do anything? Let's say that you planned a trip in a few weeks. All of the sudden, your car breaks down and you can't go on your trip, or, your car breaks down and you now have no money for the trip. Maybe you get sick and can't go. Could you have ever foreseen this? Of course not! Only God can. Therefore, instead of saying we will go, you should say, if God wills it, we will go. If God wills it, I will have a better job next year. If God wills it, we will buy a home next year. Even if it is tomorrow, you never know what tomorrow will bring. Our life is never truly in our hands. Our breath, our heartbeat, is all in His hands. As much as we try and control the things around us, they are not for us to control, but God's. He made us, He watches over us, He protects us, and He loves us. It's always Him. He is the One in control, and I wouldn't want it any other way.

James 4:16

Please read 1 Corinthians 12:15-26

We all matter. We can not say that one is greater than another. Don't you know, that the first shall be last? Do not boast in your own pride. For what you have, you only have because the Lord provided it. Or do you not remember, that all good gifts are from our Father?

James 4:17

And that servant who knew his master's will, and did not prepare himself or do according to his will, shall be beaten with many stripes. But he who did not know, yet committed things deserving of stripes, shall be beaten with few. For everyone to whom much is given, from him much will be required; and to whom much has been committed, of him they will ask the more.

Luke 12:47-48

Need I say more?

James 5:1-6

Please read Matthew 6:19-21

These scriptures in James 5 are the example of what not to do. The riches of these people are corrupted. Their riches are made in dishonest, and selfish gain. Their garments are destroyed, and their rusted and corroded money, will testify against their sins. Their flesh will be eaten like fire. The treasures that they heaped, were not treasures fit for the kingdom of heaven. They stored up treasures where moth and rust destroy. They earned their money by taking what was owed to their laborers. They committed fraud and stole from the ones who cry out. The Lord has heard their cries.

Please read Luke 16:19-31

Your time on this earth is but a breath. Eternity is forever. You have had your luxury on earth, hurting the wounded, wounding the hurt, and the time will come, for judgment upon you. As an animal is fattened before slaughter, you have fattened yourselves with the treasures of this earth. Caring for your own self, but never for the sake of others. The day of judgment will come, where you will be punished.

In God's great mercy, He offers a way out of eternal damnation, but, once the door is closed, it will be closed forever. Repent now while you still have time, and ask for the Lord's forgiveness. Recognize that you are a sinner, and believe in the death and resurrection of Jesus Christ our Lord and Savior. Only then, will you be saved.

When Jesus separates the goats from the sheep, which side will you be on?

See Matthew 25:31-46

James 5:7-8

When a farmer tills the land and sows it's seed, is the reward instant? No, because it takes time, and it takes patience. Sometimes it takes 3 months, sometimes shorter, and sometimes longer. Did you know that the slowest growing flower, according to Guinness World Records, takes 80 years or more to produce it's first set of flowers? If you are curious, it's a rare species of giant bromeliad *Puya raimondii*. Whether you are growing crops, flowers, or anything else for that matter, it takes time. Even we take time to grow. To grow from a baby to an adult, to grow spiritually and mentally, etc. We are in such a fast paced world, that we want things when we want them, however, as I have said before, God does not always work this way. Look at how long it takes from the time of conception, to the birth of a baby. It's not instant, and it takes time and patience. God is love, and love doesn't rush things. Your time will come, so be patient with the Lord, as He is patient with you. This is in regards to whatever you may be going through, as well as to the coming of the Lord. Many may wonder where He is, and why He won't come back for us already,

But, beloved, do not forget this one thing, that with the Lord one day is as a thousand years, and a thousand years as one day. The Lord is not slack concerning His promise, as some count slackness, but is longsuffering toward us, not willing that any should perish but that all should come to repentance.

2 Peter 3:8-9

God will come back for us, and He will fulfill His promises to us. He is not a God who fails to keep His word. He is a good God. The

One and Only. What we think is slow, is right on time for God. Think about it this way. I am sure many people wish God would come back already. Why can't you just take us home God? When are you coming to end our suffering? I understand the question, as I am sure that we have all thought it in some form or another. Wishing that He would come get us so we can be with Him. But, from the eyes of a loving Father, it looks different. Suppose that the first person who asked Him to come take us home, He gave them their request. Would you even be born? I think not! Suppose that someone 400 years ago asked this question, and He came back for everyone. Where would that leave you? God is not slow in keeping His promises to us, but He doesn't look at only half of the painting, He sees the whole thing. He is the wisest of wise, no one wiser than He. Only He sees this painting in it's entirety. Therefore, knowing this, we can see but a glimpse of His love for us. Knowing that He does want us with Him, He truly does. But, work still needs to be done, people still need to be born, and people still need to be saved. He wants all to come to repentance. He wants all to be saved. So yes, He does want us with Him, but only God knows when it is finished.

James 5:9

Put away your bad temper. Do you not know that anger does not produce the righteousness that the Lord desires? Do not live as the world lives. Do not get angry, complain, and judge others. We see this clearly in scriptures, through people who suffered and did not follow the world. David for example, after he had multiple opportunities to kill Saul, did not. David had every opportunity to exact revenge on the person who was trying to kill him. The one trying to take his life. He could have used the world's logic, an eye for an eye, but this, would make the whole world go blind! Instead, when Saul was in David's hands, he made the decision to leave it in God's hands. He chose to leave his problems in God's more than capable hands. Instead, he knew and believed that God would be the One to deliver him. And deliver him He did.

What about you. Do you return insults for insults? Do you do unto others as they do unto you, or do you do unto others as you would want them to do to you?

Remember, an eye for an eye, makes the whole world blind!

James 5:10

Look at the apostles. Did they not have joy in their suffering?

And they agreed with him, and when they had called for the apostles and beaten them, they commanded that they should not speak in the name of Jesus, and let them go. So they departed from the presence of the council, rejoicing that they were counted worthy to suffer shame for His name. And daily in the temple, and in every house, they did not cease teaching and preaching Jesus as the Christ.

Acts 5:40-42

They rejoiced because they were counted as worthy. Worthy to suffer shame for Jesus. They saw it as pure joy. They looked past the pain, and into the eternal. But, while they were beaten, that doesn't mean that the beating itself did not hurt. I can't speak for them, but beatings are usually painful. But, there was no mention of how badly they were beaten, who got hit where, or if they cried. Because the purpose of the passage is to look beyond the pain. Beyond the hurt. Pain never feels good while it's happening, but it does produce growth, more so if we handle it correctly. The apostles were beaten, and while it may not have been pleasant, they walked away joyful. They could have walked away bitter and angry that God allowed it to happen, but instead, they chose to see through different eyes. They chose to count it as joy that they were suffering for Christ. They could have walked away saying that they would never speak in the name of Jesus again, as this is what they were commanded, but instead, they did not cease teaching and preaching Jesus as the Christ.

I want to add that when we are suffering, our sorrow is temporary.

Now Jesus knew that they desired to ask Him, and He said to them, "Are you inquiring among yourselves about what I said, 'A little while, and you will not see Me; and again a little while, and you will see Me'? Most assuredly, I say to you that you will weep and lament, but the world will rejoice; and you will be sorrowful, but your sorrow will be turned into joy. A woman, when she is in labor, has sorrow because her hour has come; but as soon as she has given birth to the child, she no longer remembers the anguish, for joy that a human being has been born into the world. Therefore you now have sorrow; but I will see you again

and your heart will rejoice, and your joy no one will take from
you.

John 16:19-22

This passage gave us two examples. One of pain on earth turned into joy on earth, and one with pain on earth turned into joy in heaven. You don't have to wait until you get to heaven, to experience joy. God offers joy here on earth. That's one of the fruits of the Spirit for a reason. You may ask, how do you get joy?
The fruits of the Spirit are not something that you give to yourself. It comes from the Holy Spirit. The fruits are not ours to obtain, instead, they are given to us. That's why scriptures tell us to BEAR the fruit. Bearing is not producing.

"I am the true vine, and My Father is the vinedresser. Every branch in Me that does not bear fruit He takes away; and every branch that bears fruit He prunes, that it may bear more fruit. You are already clean because of the word which I have spoken to you.

John 15:1-3

The fruits of the Spirit come to you more and more as you get closer and closer to God. As you read His word, pray, and spend time with Him, you start becoming more and more like Him. You exhibit His traits, and you start bearing more and more of His fruits. This happens because God prunes the fruit. If you are not aware of what pruning is, it hurts. Pruning a tree involves removing branches. Cutting, trimming, and taking away the branches that can hinder the tree later on in it's life. If you have never seen what this looks like, please search the words, before and after pruning a tree. You will see what I mean. It looks as if someone mutilated the tree. But, it is actually helping the tree. It's removing the things that don't belong, allowing it to grow into a better, fuller tree. It will have more structural integrity, meaning that it won't so easily collapse in those areas, because you are removing the things that may fall later on in life. Some trees also require more precise trimming. Just as some of us, need more trimming than others. Pruning a tree also takes patience. If you prune too much at once, it can damage the tree, as the tree does get stressed, just as we do. Hence, when we face trials, sometimes it feels as if we get hit back, to back, to back, but remember, God knows exactly what He is doing. He knows where to apply pressure, and how much of it to apply. After all, He did make us! And, He does love us, immensely, so He never wants to hurt or damage us, but to help us grow. To help us become more and more like Jesus.

Remember, you can have joy on earth, but no joy compares to the joy that we will all have together in heaven. Right where we are meant to be, next to a loving Savior, who gave His life to save us.

James 5:11

In this scripture I am reminded of something that Job said.

Though He slay me, yet will I trust Him.

Job 13:15

He was making a statement that no matter what comes his way, he will still trust God. Many of you know the story of Job. Thinking of someone losing their children, their home, livestock, etc, is a painful story to swallow. This man loved God, yet he still had to go through trials, as do we. Losing one child is hard enough on it's own, but Job lost all 10 of his children, at once! All of these things that Job worked for, cared for, and loved, gone, in an instant. Literally back to back. Yet, he still trusted in God, despite the pain that he faced. Even his wife wanted him to curse God and die. Here we see the paths of two people. One is Job, and one is Job's wife. Two people, two paths. One that chose to be mad at God for the things that happened to her, and one that chose to trust God, even though He slayed him. In the end, Job received more than he had lost. While the memory of what was lost still remained, he chose to move forward. That doesn't mean that he didn't still miss his kids, or think about them, it just means that he made the choice to move forward. To me, this story hits home. I have kids and the thought of this hurts me. So I feel sad for what he went through. This is why I want to take a moment to say something to anyone who has lost someone that they love. Whether it's a child, a spouse, or a friend. God sees you. God hasn't left you or abandoned you. He sees your pain, He sees your hurt, and He weeps with you and for you. God has His hand on you, even if you can't see it, or feel it. I don't know who this is for, but I feel like someone needs to hear that everything is going to be OK. It may not feel like it now, and it may hurt so bad that you can't stand it, but God is with you through every bit of your pain. He sees you.

James 5:12

This verse reminds me of a verse in Matthew.

But I say to you, do not swear at all: neither by heaven, for it is God's throne; nor by the earth, for it is His footstool; nor by Jerusalem, for it is the city of the great King. Nor shall you swear by your head, because you cannot make one hair white or black. But let your 'Yes' be 'Yes,' and your 'No,' 'No.' For whatever is more than these is from the evil one.

Matthew 5:34-37

If I say, I swear by the heavens that something is true, I am swearing by something that I have no authority over. If I swear by my head, still, I have no authority to even turn a hair white or black. If I swear something to be true, and if not, let lightning strike me, again, I have no authority over that lightning bolt to strike me. This scripture is telling us that a yes should be yes and a no should be no. I have no authority to do otherwise.

James 5:13-15

The emphasis on all of these things here, is God. If you are suffering, pray to God, happy, sing to God, and if you are sick, call the elders of the church, to pray to God, while anointing him with oil in the name of the Lord. All lead to God. God should never be someone that you just go to when you are suffering or sick, but also when you are cheerful. When you are happy, God wants you to share that happiness with Him. Why? Because He loves you. If my child gets into a college, and he is so excited that he comes to me and says mom, I got into college and I wanted to tell you first, how joyful would I be? Not only that he came to me first, but that in his excitement, he thought of me. He loved me enough to share something with me that was important to him. In the same sense, God loves when we share our joy with Him. When you tell Him how happy you are for that new job He allowed you to get, the anxiety that God helped you break, or just because you're super joyful lately. He loves to share in our joy. He loves when we want to include Him in that joy. Not to mention, He is always the cause of that joy. When you don't share your joy with God, it's like you taking a gift from someone, and then running off without so much as a thank you. Without sharing with them how much you love it and how grateful that you are for that gift. I'm sure the person giving that gift would be terribly hurt by that. So is God. I believe that it truly does hurt Him when we only come to Him when we are hurting, and not for the rest. He wants to be the center of our lives in all things, not just the sad things, but the joyful things as well. God wants to be close to you, He wants to hear about your day, and about how you're feeling, the good and the bad.

The passage about calling for the elders of the church, also reminds me of this scripture below.

"Again I say to you that if two of you agree on earth concerning anything that they ask, it will be done for them by My Father in heaven. For where two or three are gathered together in My name, I am there in the midst of them."

Matthew 18:19-20

God wants us to come to others for help. This is why in Galatians 6:2, we are told to *Bear one another's burdens*.

God never intended for us to carry these burdens alone. This means that not only will Jesus give you rest, as seen in Matthew 11:28-30, but it also means that God wants to work through others to help us as well. Why? Because we are all one. Jesus is the head, and we are the body. We are supposed to be working in unity with one another, in harmony. Helping one another, lifting each other up, and bearing one another's burdens.

I also wanted to add something in regards to anointing with oil. We also see oil being used in Mark 6:13.

And they cast out many demons, and anointed with oil many who were sick, and healed them.

I could write what I think the anointing does, but to be honest, it's only an opinion. I say this because according to scriptures, we see that anointing with oil was used when people were sick, we also see it used when Samuel anointed Saul who was to be ruler in 1 Samuel 10:1, the high priest was also anointed with oil as seen in Numbers 35:25, as well as some other scriptures where we also see anointing with oil. I am not firm on my thoughts on what it is for, and it's only speculation, so I will only add this. The next verse tells us that we must have faith in the healing that we are wanting. This is why it says, *And the prayer of faith will save the sick, and the Lord will raise him up.* You have to believe that you are healed. If you don't have faith in the healing, it's like me saying, "Heal me Lord, even though I don't believe you will". So many times we see scriptures where Jesus says things like, *"Daughter, your faith has made you well. Go in peace, and be healed of your affliction."* We are given examples on what it is to have faith. A woman believing that Jesus can and will heal her, if only she touched the hem of His garment.

"If only I may touch His clothes, I shall be made well."

Mark 5:28

What about the ruler of the synagogue? The one who wanted Jesus to heal the 12 year old girl. We see Jesus responding when someone said she was dead. Jesus's response was

"Do not be afraid; only believe."

Mark 5:36

Faith. Faith requires action, but also belief.

James 5:16

We are supposed to pray for one another. If someone tells you that they are hurting, scared, sad, feel guilty, ashamed, etc, DO NOT JUDGE. We are told not to judge, and that whatever measure we use, it will be measured back to us.

For with what judgment you judge, you will be judged; and with the measure you use, it will be measured back to you.

Matthew 7:2

We are not meant to judge, but to pray. To listen, and to pray. Let me give you an example. If someone confides in you and tells you that they have been having issues with anxiety, don't respond with, well that's not Godly, fear is not of God, or it's in your head, etc. Anxiety is very real. It's so painful to go through anxiety. I know first hand what anxiety does to you. Instead, you should respond with gentleness. Realize that you can't judge what you don't understand. You could never understand what goes on inside of someone with anxiety, especially if you have never experienced it yourself. Whenever someone comes to you for help, remember these key things.

Is what I am about to say going to help, or hurt them?

Is what I am about to say going to make them feel worse about themselves or their situation?

Is what I am about to say using gentleness?

Is what I am about to say judging them in any way?

Is what I am going to say according to scripture?

And yes, some things that you want to say are according to scripture, but that doesn't mean that it's the time to say it. Remember, gentleness. It requires a certain delicacy when you are dealing with someone who is hurting. This is why it's so important to ask the Holy Spirit for guidance whenever anyone tells you anything. If you hear the words can I talk to you, can I ask your advice, can you help me with something, etc, the first thought should be, Holy Spirit, please give me the right words to say. Even if it's a quick little prayer in your head, acknowledging that you need guidance to help you say the right things, and to act in a manner pleasing to the Lord, in a manner worthy of your calling, and in a manner that will help that person. A lot of the times, someone is coming to you because they genuinely need help. Haven't you ever needed help before? Use that same gentleness that you would want someone to use towards you when you are hurting, sad, angry, depressed, anxious, worried, etc.

James 5:16-18

The effective, fervent prayer of a righteous man avails much.

James 5:16

The word fervent means having or displaying a passionate intensity.
The word passionate means showing or caused by strong feelings or a strong belief.

This means that when we pray and strongly believe that what we are praying for will happen, it produces a result that is to our benefit. Maybe spiritually, mentally, physically, eternally, or something else. Only God knows what your prayer and your belief will produce in you or for you. I say this because sometimes we pray and pray again, and we don't feel like we are getting anywhere, but we couldn't be farther from the truth. Why? Because only God knows the kind of righteousness it's producing. Maybe it's growing your faith, your persistence, your character. Maybe something is already changing but you just can't see it yet, but in time, you will. Only God knows. I say this to

61

strengthen you. To give you hope that your prayers are not for nothing, they do mean something. They mean something to God. He does hear you and He is working on things, even if you can't see it yet, in time, you will.

Elijah shows that *The effective, fervent prayer of a righteous man avails much. Elijah had a nature just like ours.* Yet, God heard him. Elijah being just a man as we are, prayed for it not to rain, and God answered him, just as He answers us. It did not rain on the land for three whole years and six months. Then, Elijah prayed again and it rained, *and the heaven gave rain, and the earth produced its fruit.* God heard His children then, and God hears His children now. It doesn't matter where you are, or what you have done, He still hears you. This was pointed out by saying that *Elijah was a man with a nature like ours.* He had a nature just like we do, yet God in His great love, compassion, and mercy, still heard him. And He hears you too. Remember that.

James 5:19-20

This shows us how important we are to the kingdom of God. God wants us to play a role in His kingdom, and this is one of the many verses in the bible that proves that. He wants us to be like Jesus. In Isaiah we are told of the prophesy of a Savior who would set the captives free.

"The Spirit of the Lord GOD is upon Me,
Because the LORD has anointed Me
To preach good tidings to the poor;

He has sent Me to heal the brokenhearted,
To proclaim liberty to the captives,
And the opening of the prison to those who are bound;
To proclaim the acceptable year of the LORD,
And the day of vengeance of our God;
To comfort all who mourn,
To console those who mourn in Zion,
To give them beauty for ashes,
The oil of joy for mourning,
The garment of praise for the spirit of heaviness;
That they may be called trees of righteousness,
The planting of the LORD, that He may be glorified."

Isaiah 61:1-3

We too are meant to lead others to that same Savior who set us free, so that He may also in turn, set them free. Whether it's the lost who don't know Him, or the hurting who have forgotten Him, we are called to lead them to Jesus, to the One who sets the captives free. So I leave you with these words.

Follow The Great Commission and *Go therefore and make disciples of all the nations, baptizing them in the name of the Father and of the Son and of the Holy Spirit, teaching them to observe all things that I have commanded you; and lo, I am with you always, even to the end of the age."* Amen.

If you would like to read more books by Tentmaker Ministries, please visit Tm-Ministries.com

www.ingramcontent.com/pod-product-compliance
Lightning Source LLC
Chambersburg PA
CBHW011218120626
46545CB00008B/3051